Suggested books and songs

Books

The Enormous Turnip, *Nicola Baxter*
(Ladybird books, hardback, 1998)

Ten Seeds, *Ruth Brown*
(Andersen press, hardback, 2001)

Fran's Flower, *Lisa Bruce* **and** *Rosalind Beardshaw*
(Bloomsbury, paperback, 2000)

Jasper's Beanstalk, *Nick Butterworth* **and** *Mick Inkpen*
(Hodder Children's Books, paperback, 1993)

The Very Hungry Caterpillar, *Eric Carle*
(Hamish Hamilton, hardback, 1994)

The Tiny Seed,
Eric Carle
(Picture Puffin,
paperback, 2001)

From Little Acorns, *Sam Godwin*
(Hodder Wayland, hardback, 2001)

Seed in Need, *Sam Godwin* **and** *Simone Abel*
(Hodder, hardback, 1998)

The Very Busy Bee, *Jack Tickle*
(Little Tiger Press, hardback, 2005)

Songs

One Man Went to Mow

Lavender Blue

In and Out the Dusky Bluebells

Little Robin Redbreast

Jingle, Jangle Scarecrow

I Had a Little Nut Tree

Round and Round the Garden
Round and round the garden
Like a teddy bear.
One step, two step, tickly under there…

Mary, Mary, Quite Contrary
Mary, Mary, quite contrary,
How does your garden grow?
With silver bells and cockle shells
And little maids all in a row.

Five Fat Peas
Five fat peas in a pea-pod pressed,
One grew, two grew, and so did all the rest.
They grew and they grew … and did not stop,
Until one day the pod went … POP!

Oats and Beans and Barley Grow
Oats and beans and barley grow,
Oats and beans and barley grow.
Do you or I or anyone know
How oats and beans and barley grow?

First the farmer sows his seed,
Then he stands and takes his ease,
Stamps his feet and claps his hands
And turns around to view the lands.

Rock-a-bye, Baby
Rock-a-bye, baby, in the tree top.
When the wind blows, the cradle will rock.
When the bough breaks, the cradle will fall,
And down will come baby, cradle and all.

Talking points

- Where do birds live?

- Flowers and plants need water and light to grow.

- There are many different types of weather – such as rain and sunshine. What other types can you think of?

- What weather do you like best?

- What colour are the leaves on the trees? (Dependent on the time of year.)

- Where might you find creepy crawlies?

- Do you have a garden at home? Who cuts the grass?

- What do different flowers and plants smell like? Do you like the smell?

- If we grow vegetables we can eat them for our lunch.

Key words

- Flowers.
- Trees.
- Leaves.

- Garden areas – grass, border, earth, patio, playground.
- Water.
- Colours.
- Size – big, small; long, short.

- Names of creepy crawlies – worm, bee, spider, caterpillar, butterfly, snail.
- Birds.
- Weather – wind, rain, sun.
- Plant pot.
- Watering can.
- Names of vegetables – carrots, potatoes.

Contents

everything
early years

Key opportunities

Our activities promote the same holistic approach to development and learning as highlighted by the Framework. All of the activities in this book promote learning through interaction with people and exploration of the world around us. However, each activity also picks up on some specific areas of the **Birth to 3 Matters** Framework.

Aspects	Components			
A Strong Child	**Me, Myself and I** *Realisation of own individuality* 4 5 6 7*	**Being Acknowledged and Affirmed** *Experiencing and seeking closeness* 5 7	**Developing Self-assurance** *Being able to trust and rely on own abilities* 1 2 3 4 6 7 9	**A Sense of Belonging** *Acquiring social confidence and competence* 1 2 3 5 7 8 9
A Skilful Communicator	**Being Together** *Being a sociable and effective communicator* 3 4 6 7	**Finding a Voice** *Being a confident and competent language user* 9	**Listening and Responding** *Listening and responding appropriately to language* 1 2 3 4 5 6 7 8 9	**Making Meaning** *Understanding and being understood* 1 6 8
A Competent Learner	**Making Connections** *Connecting ideas and understanding the world* 2 3 7 9	**Being Imaginative** *Responding to the world imaginatively* 1 5 8	**Being Creative** *Responding to the world creatively* 1 2 3 5 7 8 9	**Representing** *Responding to the world with marks and symbols* 5 6
A Healthy Child	**Emotional Well-being** *Emotional stability and resilience* 2	**Growing and Developing** *Physical well-being* 9	**Keeping Safe** *Being safe and protected* 3 4	**Healthy Choices** *Being able to make choices* 1 3 4 5 6 7 9

*These numbers refer to the Activity Sheet numbers – from page 6 onwards.

everything
early years

Planting calendar

This planting guide gives you an idea of when and what to plant during the year.
This is a good way of knowing what to plant if you wish to use the result as a present, for example, for Mothering Sunday or Easter.

	For summer flowering (Plant March–May)	For autumn flowering (Plant June–July)	For winter flowering (Plant September)
Snow drops	Daisies	Lobelia	Winter Pansies
Hyacinths	Carrots	Geraniums	
Daffodils	Cucumbers	Carrots	
Forget-me-nots	Potatoes	Dahlias	
Tulips	Peas	Begonias	
	Peppers		
	Marigolds		
	Tomatoes		
	Petunias		

Cardboard caterpillars

What you need

- *The Very Hungry Caterpillar,* Eric Carle.
- **Cardboard egg boxes.**
- **Newspaper.**
- **Brightly coloured paints.**
- **Paint brushes.**

- **Sellotape.**
- **Marker pen.**
- **Needle and cotton.**
- **Pipe cleaners (for antennae).**

Preparation

- Read the story with the children, showing them what a caterpillar looks like. Leave the book in the book corner, so they can look at it when they want.
- Cut your egg boxes into different length strips.
- Cover the area you are going to use with newspaper.
- Cut the pipe cleaners into small strips – the right size to be used as antennae.

What to do

1. Let the children choose the colours they want to paint their caterpillar.
2. Help them with the painting of the egg box strips. Let them decide how many different pieces they want to paint. Encourage them to use different colours.
3. Allow the strips to dry.
4. Once dry, use the needle and cotton to connect the separate strips of egg box into a caterpillar shape.
5. Add eyes and a mouth using the maker pen.
6. Ask the children to pick what colour they would like their antennae to be, attach these using sticky tape.
7. The caterpillars are now complete and are ready to be taken home or displayed.

Prompts

- Encourage the children to count when deciding on how many pieces to use for their caterpillar.
- Talk about long and short, showing them the difference.
- Ask the children to recognise and name the colour paints they use.
- Talk to the children about other creepy crawlies you find in the garden including spiders, worms and bees.
- Talk to the children about where you would find these – for example, under a stone, in the ground, on a flower.

everything
early years

Cress heads

What you need

- Pairs of old tights.
- Sawdust.
- Mustard seeds.
- Sheets of coloured sticky paper.
- Plastic or paper cups.
- Plastic bowl.
- Large tray – if carrying the activity out indoors.
- Small child's watering can.

Preparation

- Cut the legs off the tights, each child will need 1 leg.
- Draw and cut out of the coloured sticky paper – different face parts for the children to stick on their cress heads. For instance, sets of eyes, noses, ears and mouths.

Prompts

- Let the children play and feel the sawdust before you ask them to begin filling the heads. Talk to them and use words to describe the texture and smell.

- Encourage them to count the handfuls or cupfuls of sawdust they are using.

- Ask the children to name the different parts of the face as they decorate the cress heads. Use this as an opportunity to talk about what makes them happy or sad.

What to do

1. Pour the sawdust into the bowl.
2. Hold open the leg of the tights, and place a handful of mustard seeds in the toe end.
3. Ask the children to fill the leg with sawdust. They can use either their hands or a cup. Ensure they push the sawdust right into the toe end.
4. You need to leave enough material at the end of the leg to be able to tie the material into a knot.
5. Sit the full leg in the cup – with the seed (toe) end at the top.
6. The children can now choose from the face parts you made earlier to decorate their cress heads.
7. Finally the children need to water their cress head.
8. Place the heads in a sunny position – for instance, on a window ledge – and make sure the children water them daily.
9. Within a few days the cress will begin growing and the cress heads will then have hair!

Hints and tips

- This activity works well both indoors and out. But if you do it outdoors there is less tidying up and you can put the sawdust in an empty sand tray and carry this activity out with a larger group of children.

- Allow the children the opportunity to play in the sawdust, using it when it is both wet and dry.

everything
early years

CRAVEN COLLEGE

Leaf printing tree pictures

What you need

- **Paint.**
- **Trays for paint.**
- **Leaves of different sizes.**
- **Twigs and branches.**

- **Glue or sellotape.**
- **Large sheets of paper.**

Preparation

- Collect twigs, branches and leaves.

What to do

1. Pour a small amount of paint into the bottom of a large tray and show the children how to press the leaves into it.

2. Take the leaves out of the tray, and help the children press each leaf (paint side down) onto the sheet of paper. Gently rub the back of the leaf to get the best possible print.

3. Encourage the children to peel the leaf off gently, and then place it back on the paper and rub again.

4. Use different coloured paints and different leaves.

5. Continue dipping the leaves in the paint and then printing until each child is happy with his/her picture.

6. Allow the pictures to dry.

7. Once dry, assist the children in sticking twigs onto their picture to make a trunk for their tree. You may need to use sellotape for the larger twigs.

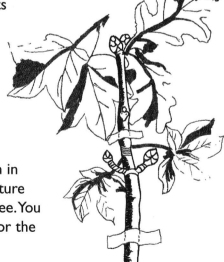

Prompts

- While collecting the leaves and twigs talk to the children about the different sizes and colours.
- Talk about the feel and texture of the leaves.
- Talk to the children about how leaves turn brown and then fall off the trees.
- If collecting in the autumn encourage the children to play leaf kicking.
- Talk about the animals that live in trees, and the noises they make.
- Ask the children to recognise and name the colours of the paints you are using.
- When making the pictures with the children recall and recount events from the walk.

Hints and tips

- If you are not in the position to take the children out for a walk to collect items, try using artificial leaves.
- Alternatively, ask the children to bring in leaves from flowers or vegetables collected from home.

everything

early years

Planting

What you need

- **A range of different sized pots.**
- **Watering cans.**
- **Labels for the pots.**
- **Bags of soil, sand and bark.**
- **Small gardening equipment – including forks, trowels and rakes.**

- **A selection of objects, seeds, plants and food for the children to plant (these should include interesting everyday objects that you know will not grow, for example: dried pasta, small toys, sweets and so on).**
- **Large trays to put the soil, sand and bark in.**

Preparation

- Ask the children to collect seeds from fruit or vegetables they have eaten at home and bring them in.
- Ask the children to bring in old clothes to wear while carrying out this activity, as they will get messy.

What to do

1. Provide the children with the pots and gardening equipment. Explain how the tools are used.

2. Assist the children with planting their items. Allow them to choose what to plant – seeds and other objects, and what they wish to plant it in – soil, bark or sand (or a combination of these).

3. Let the children play with the mud and water – making mud pies.

4. After the children have planted their items stick labels on the pots so you know what has been planted.

5. Water the pots and place them in an area where the children can visit daily to water and tend to their plants – and watch for growth!

6. Talk about which seeds are growing and which are not, and explain about the stimuli needed for growth – light and water.

Prompts

- Talk to the children about the different textures whilst handling the soil, sand and bark.
- Talk to the children about the seeds they have brought in from home, and discuss what foods they are from.
- Talk to the children about creepy crawlies that live in the garden.
- Encourage the children to count as they are counting out their seeds.

Hints and tips

- Have bowls of water for hand washing ready outside so the children can clean up before going inside.
- It is a good idea to take photos of the objects before the children plant them. Stick these pictures to the pots.
- It is helpful if the children bring in pips or seeds from food, that you provide the children with these foods to look at and plant as well.

everything
early years

Bird feeder

What you need

- **Empty yoghurt pots or plastic cups.**
- **Block of lard.**
- **Sunflower seeds.**
- **Bread.**

- **Raisins and currants.**
- **String.**
- **Glue and coloured paper – including sticky paper.**

Preparation

- Put a small hole in the bottom of the pots or cups and thread the string through them. Tie it off so the cup can hang upside down.
- Cut the coloured and sticky paper into various shapes.

Prompts

- Ask the children about the sounds birds make.
- Talk to the children about where birds live.
- Try and identify some of the birds that come to eat from the feeder.
- Encourage turn taking when adding the ingredients into the pan.
- Recite **Two Little Dickie Birds** with the children.

What to do

1. Melt the lard, and allow the pan to cool, away from the children
2. While this is happening, help the children decorate their cups, so they will know which one is theirs when they are hanging up.
3. Ask the children to help add the seeds, bread, raisins and currants to the pan of melted lard.
4. Stir all the ingredients together.
5. Assist the children in spooning the mixture into the cups, pushing it down firmly.
6. Allow the mixture to cool and set in the cups.
7. Once set, hang the pots outside and wait for the birds!

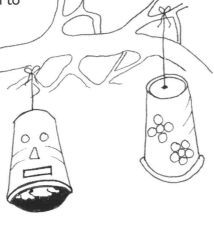

Hints and tips

- When making bird feeders and using seeds you should be allergy aware. Never use nuts.
- When hanging the feeders ensure the children will have a clear view of the birds but that they are not able to reach the feeders.
- Feeders are a nice idea to send home and will encourage parents to explore the garden with their children.

everything
early years

Windmills

What you need

- **Sheets of coloured paper.**
- **Shiny paper and tissue paper.**
- **Crayons.**
- **Glue.**
- **Thin garden stakes.**
- **Paper fasteners.**

Preparation

- On one of the square pieces of paper draw 2 diagonal lines – one to each of 2 corners.
- Cut the shiny paper into small pieces.

What to do

1. Help the children to decorate, using shiny or tissue paper, their square pieces of paper. Alternatively, they could just colour them.

2. Cut along the diagonal lines stopping 2cm from the middle on all four lines.

3. Bend the right hand top and bottom corners into the middle, followed by the left hand top and bottom corners (a).

4. Make a small hole in the middle of the square and carefully secure each flap with a paper fastener (b).

5. Attach the paper fastener to a garden stake, you may need to use sellotape for this.

6. Show how the windmill goes round by blowing it, or take the children into the garden if it is a windy day.

(a)   (b)

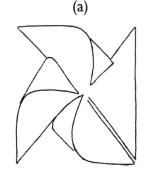 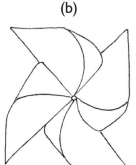

Prompts

- Talk to the children about the weather – particularly about the wind.
- Ask the children to name the colours they are using while decorating their windmill.
- Use words to describe the action of the windmill, for example: turning, spinning, round and round.
- Recite the nursery rhyme **Rock a Bye Baby**, with the children.

Hints and tips

- If you laminate the sheets of paper after the children have decorated them – and before you cut down the lines – it will make the windmills more water proof.
- You can vary the size of paper you use, but larger windmills will not work as well as they need more wind to make them rotate.

everything
early years

Gardening in a jar

What you need

- **Large glass jars or bowls with lids (the jar must be big enough to fit your hand into).**
- **Compost.**
- **Soil.**
- **Gravel.**
- **Small house plants – such as begonias, japonicas.**

Prompts

- Talk to children about the colour of the plants they choose.
- Talk to them about the feel and texture of the different materials used.
- Count with the children as they add the spoons of gravel and soil to the jar, also count the plants.
- Talk about the different sizes of the plants using words such as big and small. Also use words to describe the texture of the soil – such as wet and damp.
- While carrying out this activity use words to describe the actions they are using, for example: digging, planting and watering.

Preparation

- Collect together all you need and make sure you can fit your hand inside the jar with ease (and take it out!).

What to do

1. Help the children to put a layer of gravel in the bottom of the jar.
2. Let the children mix together some soil and compost, use this to add a layer on top of the gravel.
3. Pat the soil down.
4. Allow the children to dig in the soil – using the spoon to make some holes.
5. Ask the children to pick which plants they want to use, and assist them in planting these in the jar.
6. Water the plants well and place the lid on the jar.
7. Stand the gardens in a bright place or on a window sill within easy sight of the children. Water them regularly.

Hints and tips

- If the jar steams up and becomes cloudy take the lid off for a few minutes and it will clear.
- Allow the children to water regularly but limit the amount of water so they do not over water the gardens.
- Don't use ferns for this activity – as they grow too quickly and over power the other plants.

everything

early years

Scarecrow

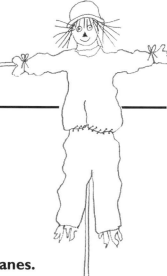

© Copyright Everything Early Years 2005. All rights reserved

What you need

- An old pair of children's trousers and an old jumper.
- Old hat.
- Newspaper.
- String.

- Bag of straw.
- Permanent maker.
- Old pair of tights.
- Needle and thread.
- Two small garden canes.

Preparation

- Tie off the bottoms of the trousers and arms of the jumper with the string.

What to do

1. Show the children how to screw the newspaper up and ask them to stuff the legs of the trousers and the jumper with it.
2. Once they are full take the needle and thread and attach the jumper to the trousers.
3. Fill the end of one leg of the tights to make the head of the scarecrow.
4. Put the left over leg and rest of the tights in the neck of the jumper and secure with the needle and thread.
5. Draw a face on the scarecrow.
6. The children should help you add the hat to the scarecrow and put some straw underneath it for hair.
7. Lash the 2 canes together to create a cross.
8. Secure the scarecrow's body to the cane cross – stretching the arms of the jumper along the horizontal cane.
9. Take the scarecrow outside and stand him up using the garden cane pushed into the ground as support.

Prompts

- Ask the children to name the items of clothing you use to make the scarecrow.
- Tell the children we use scarecrows to keep the birds from eating the plants.
- Ask the children what they like to eat.
- When drawing the face on the scarecrow, talk to the children about emotions and what makes them happy and sad.

Hints and tips

- Depending on the space you have available you may decide to make a larger scarecrow, for this you will need adult sized clothing and stronger canes.
- Some children may be unsure of the scarecrow at first. Reassure the children it is a happy scarecrow and going to help look after their plants.
- It is a nice idea to ask the children to name the scarecrow.

Herb garden

What you need

- **An area outside or a large plant pot.**
- **A range of different herbs and fragrant plants, some of these can be grown from seeds and some can be developed plants.**
- **Soil and compost.**
- **Watering can.**
- **Child size gardening tools – metal ones for the older children, and plastic ones for the youngest.**

Preparation

- Ensure you have all you need – and that it is close at hand.
- Prepare a bowl of water, ready for hand washing after the activity.

What to do

1. Assist the children in planting the seeds and plants, encouraging them to use the tools correctly.
2. Encourage the children to gently rub and smell the plants as they plant them.
3. Bed the plants in well.
4. Water the plants.
5. Encourage the children to carry on watering the plants, and monitor their growth.

Prompts

- Use words to describe the fragrance of the plants to the children.
- Talk about the colour of the plants you have used.
- Talk to the children about butterflies and bees liking the colour of plants.
- Encourage the children to count the plants or seeds during the activity.

Hints and tips

- Most supermarkets now stock a range of fresh herb plants which you can use for your developed plants. Here are some plants and herbs which are particularly fragrant:

    Lavender.

    Mint.

    Curry plant.

    Lemon grass.

    Basil.

    Citrus plants.

    Oregano.

    Thyme.

    Sage.

    Rosemary.

    Chocolate cosmos.

- For further information on other plants ask at your local garden centre.

everything

early years

Display ideas

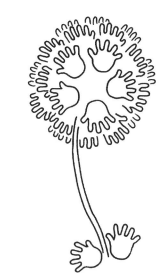

Sunflowers

For this display make sunflowers using children's yellow hand prints – cutting around them and using them as the petals. Alternatively, you could sponge paint some petals. Screw up and stick pieces of brown tissue paper to use as the centre of the flower. Cut out some stems from bright green paper.

Mary, Mary Quite Contrary

Use the nursery rhyme as your inspiration. Display rows of silver bells made from shiny paper, collect shells and use these as the cockle shells. Make this display 3-dimensional by adding tissue paper flowers you have made with the children and adding a child size watering can which Mary can hold.

A giant Very Hungry Caterpillar

Display pictures of all the food the caterpillar eats during the story. Make a caterpillar by asking each of the children to decorate a paper plate using yellow and green paint. Staple the plates to make the body of the caterpillar. Add a face.

When putting the caterpillar up on the wall make the display 3-dimensional by hanging butterflies from the ceiling in front.

Flower stall

Make a range of tissue paper flowers with the children. You could also include a range of artificial and plastic flowers in the display. Make this display 3-dimensional by bending sheets of card round and attaching to the display so they stand out to make the buckets for the flowers to stand in. Make a stripy canopy for your stall, from a collage of red and white material.

Role play corner

You can change your home corner or role play area into something exciting which is linked with the gardening theme. Make the most of outside areas, and all the space available to you – a themed corner can be really effective. Here are a few ideas.

Flower shop

Make tissue paper flowers with the children and arrange in buckets. You can also use flower baskets, plastic pots and vases. Include a till and a telephone to take orders and collect plastic and paper money. Make ribbons and bows available for decorating your bouquets.

Garden centre

Once again you can make tissue paper flowers with the children and display, along with some pictures of plants and flowers. You could also use artificial flowers and plants. There is a range of other items you could place in the role play corner to encourage play: a till, packets of seeds (laminated so they last), old clean wellies, watering cans, various pots (plastic ones are more durable), small gardening utensils, gardening books and magazines and children's plastic garden furniture.

Mary, Mary Quite Contrary's garden

You can use the display of Mary's garden which you have made with the children as a backdrop to the role play area. Also include the following items: watering cans, plastic flowers and pots, aprons, baskets, hats, shells, gardening gloves and bells.

Trays of grass

Fill trays with soil and then sprinkle on grass seed. Water the seed and place in a warm area. Once the grass has grown allow the children to use the trays of grass to play with their toy animals on.

everything
early years